Quotes About Change
Short Quotes-
Motivational Quotes ,
Inspirational Quotes

AF480128

# <u>PREFACE</u>

Let's discover together 100 short motivational and positive quotes about change , that should boost your daily life and help you take action.

Whether it's changing your attitude or trying something new, here are our top five reasons why change can bring us a better life.

1. Change puts positive in our life.

2. Change helps us stay fit.

3. It's good for mental health.

4. It can make us perform better at work.

5. Change helps us stay alert.

Most of us have dreams, goals to achieve. And we all seek happiness, even if it is different for everyone.

In these existential quests, the obstacles are numerous and discouragement falls on us at any time.

Whether we are going through a good or difficult period, in both cases, encouragement is always welcome and this is where positive and motivating quotes take on their full meaning.

In response to the demands of the reader, an attempt has been made to put in one box the immortal quotes about change scattered around. It will hopefully satisfy the reader to find in one book the quotes which have crossed the boundaries of countries and eras and become immortal. These poems have played a special role in the development of our minds and the formation of society through the ages - let's hope they will be equally useful for future generations. So if you keep this book, it will be useful for family and friends and I will consider all the efforts of making this book worthwhile.

Regards-

Editor.

Just when I think I have
learned the way to live, life
changes.

~ Hugh Prather

There are no permanent
changes because change
itself is permanent.

~Ralph L. Woods

To live is to change, and to
be perfect is to change often.

~ John Henry Cardinal
Newman

Life is about change.
Sometimes it's painful.
Sometimes it's beautiful.
But most of the time, it's
both.

~ Lana Lang

They must change often,
who would be constant in
happiness.

~ Confucius

One must never lose time in vainly regretting the past or in complaining against the changes which cause us discomfort, for change is the essence of life.

~Anatole France

To improve is to change; to
be perfect is to change often.

~ *Winston Churchill*

To exist is to change, to
change is to mature, to
mature is to go on creating
oneself endlessly.

~ *Henri Bergson*

You can't go back and
change the beginning, but
you can start where you are
and change the ending.

~ C.S. Lewis

The art of life lies in a
constant readjustment to our
surroundings.

~ Kakuzo Okakura

Progress is impossible
without change, and those
who cannot change their
minds cannot change
anything.

~ George Bernard Shaw

It is not the strongest of the species that survive, nor the most intelligent, but the one most responsive to change.

~ Charles Darwin

The measure of intelligence
is the ability to change.

~ Albert Einstein

The world as we have
created it is a process of our
thinking. It cannot be
changed without changing
our thinking.

~Albert Einstein

I've learned that you'll
never be disappointed if you
always keep an eye on
uncharted territory, where
you'll be challenged and
growing and having fun.

~ Kirstie Alley

The greatest discovery of all
time is that a person can
change his future by merely
changing his attitude.

~ Oprah Winfrey

The snake which cannot cast
its skin has to die. As well
the minds which are
prevented from changing
their opinions; they cease to
be mind.

~ Friedrich Nietzsche

I cannot say whether things
will get better if we change;
what I can say is they must
change if they are to get
better.

~Georg C. Lichtenberg

The secret of change is to
focus all of your energy not
on fighting the old, but on
building the new.

~Socrates

Let him that would move the
world first move himself.

~Socrates

When we are no longer able
to change a situation, we are
challenged to change
ourselves.

~ Viktor Frankl

How wonderful it is that
nobody need wait a single
moment before starting to
improve the world.

~ Anne Frank

The world hates change, yet
it is the only thing that has
brought progress.

~ Charles F. Kettering

We change, whether we like
it or not.

~ *Ralph Waldo Emerson*

Your life does not get better
by chance, it gets better by
change.

~ Jim Rohn

Life belongs to the living,
and he who lives must be
prepared for changes.

~ Johann Wolfgang von
Goethe

The one unchangeable
certainty is that nothing is
certain or unchangeable.

~ John F. Kennedy

One day spent with someone
you love can change
everything.

~Mitch Albom

The price of doing the same
old thing is far higher than
the price of change.


~ Bill Clinton

Times and conditions
change so rapidly that we
must keep our aim
constantly focused on the
future.

~ *Walt Disney*

No matter how far you have
gone on a wrong road, turn
back.

~ *Turkish proverb*

Growth is painful. Change
is painful. But nothing is as
painful as staying stuck
somewhere you don't belong.

~ Mandy Hale

It's okay to be scared.
Being scared means you're
about to do something really,
really brave.

~ Mandy Hale

Because things are the way
they are, things will not stay
the way they are.

~ Bertolt Brecht

Be the change that you wish
to see in the world.

~ Mahatma Gandhi

The only way to make sense
out of change is to plunge
into it, move with it, and join
the dance.

~ Alan W. Watts

All changes, even the most
longed for, have their
melancholy, for what we
leave behind us is a part of
ourselves; we must die to
one life before we can enter
into another.

~Anatole France

If you don't like something,
change it. If you can't
change it, change your
attitude.

~ Maya Angelou

Stepping onto a brand-new
path is difficult, but not more
difficult than remaining in a
situation, which is not
nurturing to the whole
woman.

~ Maya Angelou

Everyone thinks of changing
the world, but no one thinks
of changing himself.

~ Leo Tolstoy

True life is lived when tiny
changes occur.

~ Leo Tolstoy

Become a student of change.
It is the only thing that will
remain constant.

~ Anthony D'Angelo

Change will not come if we
wait for some other person
or some other time. We are
the ones we've been waiting
for. We are the change that
we seek.

~ Barack Obama

Life will only change when
you become more committed
to your dreams than you are
to your comfort zone.

~ Billy Cox

Life is measured by the
rapidity of change, the
succession of influences that
modify the being.

~ George Eliot

All is change; all yields its
place and goes.

~ Euripides

Those who expect moments
of change to be comfortable
and free of conflict have not
learned their history.

~ Joan Wallach Scott

When you're through
changing, you're through.

~ Bruce Barton

Embrace uncertainty. Some
of the most beautiful chapters
in our lives won't have a title
until much later.

~ Bob Goff

When it feels scary to jump,
that's exactly WHEN you
jump. Otherwise you end up
staying in the same place
your whole life. And that I
can't do.

~ Oscar Isaacs

Everything flows, nothing
stays still.

~ Heraclitus

It is changing that things
find purpose.

~ Heraclitus

The art of progress is to
preserve order amid change,
and to preserve change amid
order.

~ Alfred North Whitehead

Change is the law of life,
and those who look only to
the past and present are
certain to miss the future.

~John F. Kennedy

Change is inevitable in a progressive society. Change is constant.

~ Benjamin Disraeli

Every saint has a past, and
every sinner has a future.

~ Oscar Wilde

Life is a series of natural
and spontaneous changes.
Don't resist them; that only
creates sorrow. Let reality
be reality.

~ Lao Tzu

In embracing Change,
entrepreneurs ensure social
and economic stability.

~ George Gilder

You must change in order to
survive.

~ Pearl Bailey

We cannot become what we
want by remaining what we
are.

~ Max Depree

Change does not change
tradition. It strengthens it.
Change is a challenge and
an opportunity, not a threat.

~ Prince Philip of England

I can't change the direction
of the wind, but I can adjust
my sails to always reach my
destination.

~ Jimmy Dean

For many men, the
acquisition of wealth does
not end their troubles, it only
changes them.

~ Marcus Annaeus Seneca

Incredible change happens
in your life when you decide
to take control of what you
do have power over instead
of craving control over what
you don't.

~Steve Maraboli

I find the best way to love
someone is not to change
them, but instead, help them
reveal the greatest version of
themselves.

~Steve Maraboli

Change is the only evidence
of life.

~ Evelyn Waugh

Your desire to change must
be greater than your desire
to stay the same.

~ Anon.

If it doesn't challenge you, it
won't change you.

~Anon.

All great changes are
preceded by chaos.

~ Anon.

Don't make a change too
complicated, just begin.

~ Anon.

Small changes eventually
add up to huge results.

~Anon.

You can't change what's
going on around you until
you start changing what's
going on within you.

~ Anon.

When in doubt, choose change.

~ Lily Leung

I have accepted fear as part
of life — specifically the fear
of change... I have gone
ahead despite the pounding
in the heart that says, 'turn
back.'

~ Erica Jong

Yesterday I was clever, so
I wanted to change the
world. Today I am wise, so
I am changing myself.

*~ Rumi*

I alone cannot change the
world, but I can cast a stone
across the waters to create
many ripples.

~ Mother Teresa

Continuity gives us roots;
change gives us branches,
letting us stretch and grow
and reach new heights.

~ Pauline R. Kezer

Some changes look negative
on the surface but you will
soon realize that space is
being created in your life for
something new to emerge.

~ Eckhart Tolle

All love shifts and changes.
I don't know if you can be
wholeheartedly in love all the
time.

~ Julie Andrews

Things don't have to change
the world to be important.

~Steve Jobs

The people who are crazy
enough to think they can
change the world are the
ones who do.

~Steve Jobs

There is change in all
things. You yourself are
subject to continual change
and some decay and this is
common to the entire
universe.

~ Marcus Aurelius

Things do not change; we change.

~Henry David Thoreau

Any change, even a change
for the better, is always
accompanied by drawbacks
and discomforts.

~ Arnold Bennett

Turbulence is a life force. It
is an opportunity. Let's love
turbulence and use it for
change.

~ Ramsey Clark

Every day the clock resets.
Your wins don't matter.
Your failures don't matter.
Don't stress on what was,
fight for what could be.

~Sean Higgins

One child, one teacher, one
pen, and one book can change
the world.

~ Malala Yousafzai

Readjusting is a painful
process, but most of us need
it at one time or another.

~ Arthur Chirstopher
Benson

Life is change. Growth is
optional. Choose wisely.

~Karen Kaiser Clark

Everything passes;
everything wears out;
everything breaks.

~ French Proverb

Every great dream begins
with a dreamer. Always
remember, you have within
you the strength, the
patience, and the passion to
reach for the stars to change
the world.

~ Harriet Tubman

Play to your strengths. If
you aren't great at
something, do more of what
you're great
at.

~Jason Lemkin

If you can't fly, then run. If
you can't run, then walk. If
you can't walk, then crawl.
But whatever you do, you
have to keep moving
forward.

~Martin Luther King. Jr.

Change your thoughts and
you change your world.

~ Norman Vincent Peale

Just take any step, whether small or large. And then another and repeat day after day. It may take months, maybe years, but the path to success will become clear.

~ Aaron Ross

You never change things by
fighting the existing reality.
To change something, build
a new model that makes the
existing model obsolete.

~ Buckminster Fuller

Change the way you look at
things and the things you
look at change.

~ Wayne W. Dyer

The changes we dread most
may contain our salvation.

~ *Barbara Kingsolver*

And that is how change happens. One gesture. One person. One moment at a time.

~ Libba Bray

One day or day one. You
decide.

~ Anon.

# Motivational Quotes For Success

Collection Of-
Short Quotes,
Inspirational Quotes

# Quotes About Life

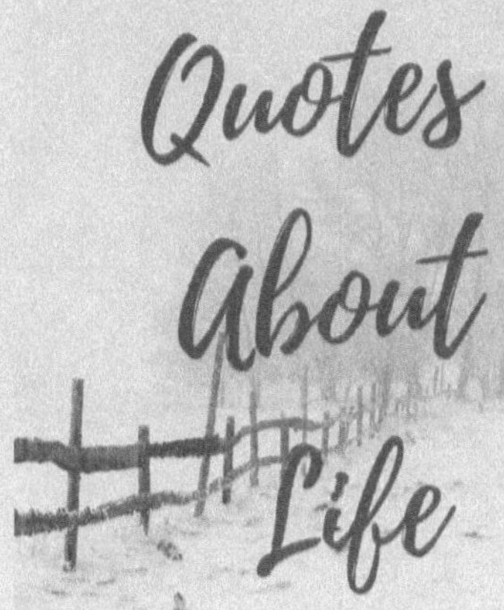

**Inspirational Quotes For a Better Life - Getting Out Of Stress, Frustration And Depression**

*Illustrated by-*
*Debopam Rai Chaudhuri*

Short Quotes
Inspirational
Quotes -About
Leadership